Variable Annuities

Variable annuities have become a part of the retirement and investment plans of many Americans. Before you buy a variable annuity, you should know some of the basics— and be prepared to ask your insurance agent, broker, financial planner, or other financial professional lots of questions about whether a variable annuity is right for you.

This is a general description of variable annuities—what they are, how they work, and the charges you will pay. Before buying any variable annuity, however, you should find out about the particular annuity you are considering. Request a prospectus from the insurance company or from your financial professional, and read it carefully. The prospectus contains important information about the annuity contract, including fees and charges, investment options, death benefits, and annuity payout options. You should compare the benefits and costs of the annuity to other variable annuities and to other types of investments, such as mutual funds.

U.S. Securities and Exchange Commission
Office of Investor Education and Advocacy
100 F Street, NE
Washington, DC 20549-0213
Telephone: (800) 732-0330
www.investor.gov

Table of Contents

What Is a Variable Annuity?

A variable annuity is a contract between you and an insurance company, under which the insurer agrees to make periodic payments to you, beginning either immediately or at some future date. You purchase a variable annuity contract by making either a single purchase payment or a series of purchase payments.

A variable annuity offers a range of investment options. The value of your investment as a variable annuity owner will vary depending on the performance of the investment options you choose. The investment options for a variable annuity are typically mutual funds that invest in stocks, bonds, money market instruments, or some combination of the three.

Although variable annuities are typically invested in mutual funds, variable annuities differ from mutual funds in several important ways:

FIRST, variable annuities let you receive **periodic payments** for the rest of your life (or the life of your spouse or any other person you designate). This feature offers protection against the possibility that, after you retire, you will outlive your assets.

SECOND, variable annuities have a **death benefit**. If you die before the insurer has started making payments to you, your beneficiary is guaranteed to receive a specified amount—typically at least the amount of your purchase payments. Your beneficiary will get a benefit from this feature if, at the time of your death, your account value is less than the guaranteed amount.

THIRD, variable annuities are tax-deferred. That means you pay no taxes on the income and investment gains from your annuity until you withdraw your money. You may also transfer your money from one investment option to another within a variable annuity without paying tax at the time of the transfer. When you take your money out of a variable annuity, however, you will be taxed on the earnings at ordinary income tax rates

Other investment vehicles, such as IRAs and employer-sponsored 401(k) plans, also may provide you with tax-deferred growth and other tax advantages. For most investors, it will be advantageous to make the maximum allowable contributions to IRAs and 401(k) plans before investing in a variable annuity.

In addition, if you are investing in a variable annuity through a tax-advantaged retirement plan (such as a 401(k) plan or an IRA), you will get no additional tax advantage from the variable annuity. Under these circumstances, consider buying a variable annuity only if it makes sense because of the annuity's other features, such as lifetime income payments and death protection. The tax rules that apply to variable annuities can be complicated—before investing, you may want to consult a tax adviser about the tax consequences to you of investing in a variable annuity.

Remember

Variable annuities are designed to be long-term investments, to meet retirement and other long-range goals. Variable annuities are not suitable for meeting short-term goals because substantial taxes and insurance company charges may apply if you withdraw your money early. Variable annuities also involve investment risks, just as mutual funds do.

rather than lower capital gains rates. In general, the benefits of tax deferral will outweigh the costs of a variable annuity only if you hold it as a long-term investment to meet retirement and other long-range goals.

How Variable Annuities Work

A variable annuity has two phases: an accumulation phase and a payout phase.

THE ACCUMULATION PHASE

During the accumulation phase, you make purchase payments, which you can allocate to a number of investment options. For example, you could designate 40% of your purchase payments to a bond fund, 40% to a U.S. stock fund, and 20% to an international stock fund. The money you have allocated to each mutual fund investment option will increase or decrease over time, depending on the fund's performance. In addition, variable annuities often allow you to allocate part of your purchase payments to a fixed account. A fixed account, unlike a mutual fund, pays a fixed rate of interest. The insurance company may reset this interest rate periodically, but it will usually provide a guaranteed minimum (e.g., 3% per year).

Your most important source of information about a variable annuity's investment options is the prospectus. Request the prospectuses for the mutual fund investment options. Read them carefully before you allocate your purchase payments among the investment options offered. You should consider a

---

EXAMPLE

You purchase a variable annuity with an initial purchase payment of $10,000. You allocate 50% of that purchase payment ($5,000) to a bond fund, and 50% ($5,000) to a stock fund. Over the following year, the stock fund has a 10% return, and the bond fund has a 5% return. At the end of the year, your account has a value of $10,750 ($5,500 in the stock fund and $5,250 in the bond fund), minus fees and charges.

---

variety of factors with respect to each fund option, including the fund's investment objectives and policies, management fees and other expenses that the fund charges, the risks and volatility of the fund, and whether the fund contributes to the diversification of your overall investment portfolio. The SEC's online publication, *Mutual Fund Investing: Look at More Than a Fund's Past Performance*, provides information about these factors. Another SEC publication, *Invest Wisely: An Introduction to Mutual Funds*, provides general information about the types of mutual funds and the expenses they charge.

During the accumulation phase, you can typically transfer your money from one investment option to another without paying tax on your investment income and gains, although you may be charged by the insurance company for transfers. However, if you withdraw money from your account during the early years of the accumulation phase, you may have to pay "surrender charges," which are discussed below. In addition, you may have to pay a 10% federal tax penalty if you withdraw money before the age of 59½.

THE PAYOUT PHASE

At the beginning of the payout phase, you may receive your purchase payments plus investment income and gains (if any) as a lump-sum payment, or you may choose to receive them as a stream of payments at regular intervals (generally monthly).

If you choose to receive a stream of payments, you may have a number of choices of how long the payments will last. Under most annuity contracts, you can choose to have your annuity payments last for a period that you set (such as 20 years) or for an indefinite period (such as your lifetime or the lifetime of you and your spouse or other beneficiary). During the payout phase, your annuity contract may permit you to choose between receiving payments that are fixed in amount or payments that vary based on the performance of the mutual fund investment options.

The amount of each periodic payment will depend, in part, on the time period that you select for receiving payments. Be aware that some annuities do not allow you to withdraw money from your account once you have started receiving regular annuity payments.

In addition, some annuity contracts are structured as immediate annuities, which means that there is no accumulation phase and you will start receiving annuity payments right after you purchase the annuity.

The Death Benefit and Other Features

A common feature of variable annuities is the death benefit. If you die, a person you select as a beneficiary (such as your spouse or child) will receive the greater of: (i) all the money in your account, or (ii) some guaranteed minimum (such as all purchase payments minus prior withdrawals).

Some variable annuities allow you to choose a "stepped-up" death benefit. Under this feature, your guaranteed minimum death benefit may be based on a greater amount than purchase payments minus withdrawals. For example, the guaranteed minimum might be your account value as of a specified date, which may be greater than purchase payments minus withdrawals if the underlying investment options have performed well. The purpose of a stepped-up death benefit is to "lock in" your investment performance and prevent a later decline in the value of your account from eroding the amount that you expect to leave to your heirs. This feature carries a charge, however, which will reduce your account value.

Variable annuities sometimes offer other optional features, which also have extra charges. One common feature, the

---

EXAMPLE

You own a variable annuity that offers a death benefit equal to the greater of account value or total purchase payments minus withdrawals. You have made purchase payments totaling $50,000. In addition, you have withdrawn $5,000 from your account. Because of these withdrawals and investment losses, your account value is currently $40,000. If you die, your designated beneficiary will receive $45,000 (the $50,000 in purchase payments you put in minus $5,000 in withdrawals).

guaranteed minimum income benefit, guarantees a particular minimum level of annuity payments, even if you do not have enough money in your account (perhaps because of investment losses) to support that level of payments. Other features may include long-term care insurance, which pays for home health care or nursing home care if you become seriously ill.

You may want to consider the financial strength of the insurance company that sponsors any variable annuity you are considering buying. This can affect the company's ability to pay any benefits that are greater than the value of your account in mutual fund investment options, such as a death benefit, guaranteed minimum income benefit, long-term care benefit, or amounts you have allocated to a fixed account investment option.

Variable Annuity Charges

You will pay several charges when you invest in a variable annuity. Be sure you understand all the charges before you invest. These charges will reduce the value of your account and the return on your investment. Often, they will include the following:

Surrender charges

If you withdraw money from a variable annuity within a certain period after a purchase payment (typically within six to eight years, but sometimes as long as ten years), the insurance company usually will assess a "surrender" charge, which is a type of sales charge. This charge is used to pay your financial professional a commission for selling the variable annuity to you. Generally, the surrender charge is a percentage of the amount withdrawn, and declines gradually over a period of several years, known as the "surrender period." For example, a 7% charge might apply in the first year after a purchase payment, 6% in the second year, 5% in the third year, and so on until the eighth year, when the surrender charge no longer applies. Often, contracts will allow you to withdraw part of your account value each year—10% or

---

EXAMPLE

You purchase a variable annuity contract with a $10,000 purchase payment. The contract has a schedule of surrender charges, beginning with a 7% charge in the first year, and declining by 1% each year. In addition, you are allowed to withdraw 10% of your contract value each year free of surrender charges. In the first year, you decide to withdraw $5,000, or one-half of your contract value of $10,000 (assuming that your contract value has not increased or decreased because of investment performance). In this case, you could withdraw $1,000 (10% of contract value) free of surrender charges, but you would pay surrender charge of 7%, or $280, on the other $4,000 withdrawn.

15% of your account value, for example—without paying a surrender charge.

Mortality and expense risk charge

This charge is equal to a certain percentage of your account value, typically in the range of 1.25% per year. This charge compensates the insurance company for insurance risks it assumes under the annuity contract. Profit from the mortality and expense risk charge is sometimes used to pay the insurer's costs of selling the variable annuity, such as a commission paid to your financial professional for selling the variable annuity to you.

> **EXAMPLE**
>
> Your variable annuity has a mortality and expense risk charge at an annual rate of 1.25% of account value. Your average account value during the year is $20,000 so you will pay $250 in mortality and expense risk charges that year.

Administrative fees

The insurer may deduct charges to cover record-keeping and other administrative expenses. This may be charged as a flat account maintenance fee (perhaps $25 or $30 per year) or as a percentage of your account value (typically in the range of 0.15% per year).

> **EXAMPLE**
>
> Your variable annuity charges administrative fees at an annual rate of 0.15% of account value. Your average account value during the year is $50,000. You will pay $75 in administrative fees.

Underlying Fund Expenses

You will also indirectly pay the fees and expenses imposed by the mutual funds that are the underlying investment options for your variable annuity.

Fees and Charges for Other Features

Special features offered by some variable annuities, such as a stepped-up death benefit, a guaranteed minimum income benefit, or long-term care insurance, often carry additional fees and charges.

Other charges, such as initial sales loads, or fees for transferring part of your account from one investment option to another, may also apply. You should ask your financial professional to explain to you all charges that may apply. You can also find a description of the charges in the prospectus for any variable annuity that you are considering.

Tax-Free "1035" Exchanges

Section 1035 of the U.S. tax code allows you to exchange an existing variable annuity contract for a new annuity contract without paying any tax on the income and investment gains in your current variable annuity account. These tax-free exchanges, known as 1035 exchanges, can be useful if another annuity has features that you prefer, such as a larger death benefit, different annuity payout options, or a wider selection of investment choices.

You may, however, be required to pay surrender charges on the old annuity if you are still in the surrender charge period. In addition, a new surrender charge period generally begins when you exchange into the new annuity. This means that, for a significant number of years (as many as 10 years), you typically will have to pay a surrender charge (which can be as high as 9% of your purchase payments) if you withdraw funds from the new annuity. Further, the new annuity may have higher annual fees and charges than the old annuity, which will reduce your returns.

CAUTION!

If you are thinking about a 1035 exchange, you should compare both annuities carefully. Unless you plan to hold the new annuity for a significant amount of time, you may be better off keeping the old annuity because the new annuity typically will impose a new surrender charge period. Also, if you decide to do a 1035 exchange, you should talk to your financial professional or tax adviser to make sure the exchange will be tax-free. If you surrender the old annuity for cash and then buy a new annuity, you will have to pay tax on the surrender.

Bonus Credits

Some insurance companies are now offering variable annuity contracts with "bonus credit" features. These contracts promise to add a bonus to your contract value based on a specified percentage (typically ranging from 1% to 5%) of purchase payments.

EXAMPLE

You purchase a variable annuity contract that offers a bonus credit of 3% on each purchase payment. You make a purchase payment of $20,000. The insurance company issuing the contract adds a bonus of $600 to your account.

CAUTION!

Variable annuities with bonus credits may carry a downside, however—higher expenses that can outweigh the benefit of the bonus credit offered.

Frequently, insurers will charge you for bonus credits in one or more of the following ways:

Higher surrender charges

Surrender charges may be higher for a variable annuity that pays you a bonus credit than for a similar contract with no bonus credit.

Longer surrender periods

Your purchase payments may be subject to surrender charges for a longer period than they would be under a similar contract with no bonus credit.

Higher mortality and expense risk charges and other charges

Higher annual mortality and expense risk charges may be deducted for a variable annuity that pays you a bonus credit. Although the difference may seem small, over time it can add up. In addition, some contracts may impose a separate fee specifically to pay for the bonus credit.

Before purchasing a variable annuity with a bonus credit, ask yourself—and the financial professional who is trying to sell you the contract—whether the bonus is worth more to you than any increased charges you will pay for the bonus. This may depend on a variety of factors, including the amount of the bonus credit and the increased charges, how long you hold your annuity contract, and the return on the underlying investments. You also need to consider the other features of the annuity to determine whether it is a good investment for you.

EXAMPLE

You make purchase payments of $10,000 in Annuity A and $10,000 in Annuity B. Annuity A offers a bonus credit of 4% on your purchase payment, and deducts annual charges totaling 1.75%. Annuity B has no bonus credit and deducts annual charges totaling 1.25%. Let's assume that both annuities have an annual rate of return, prior to expenses, of 10%. By the tenth year, your account value in Annuity A will have grown to $22,978. But your account value in Annuity B will have grown more, to $23,136, because Annuity B deducts lower annual charges, even though it does not offer a bonus.

You should also note that a bonus may only apply to your initial premium payment, or to premium payments you make within the first year of the annuity contract. Further, under some annuity contracts the insurer will take back all bonus payments made to you within the prior year or some other specified period if you make a withdrawal, if a death benefit is paid to your beneficiaries upon your death, or in other circumstances.

CAUTION!

If you already own a variable annuity and are thinking of exchanging it for a different annuity with a bonus feature you should be careful. Even if the surrender period on your current annuity contract has expired, a new surrender period generally will begin when you exchange that contract for a new one. This means that by exchanging your contract, you will forfeit your ability to withdraw money from your account without incurring substantial surrender charges. And as described above, the schedule of surrender charges and other fees may be higher on the variable annuity with the bonus credit than they were on the annuity that you exchanged.

EXAMPLE

You currently hold a variable annuity with an account value of $20,000, which is no longer subject to surrender charges. You exchange that annuity for a new variable annuity, which pays a 4% bonus credit and has a surrender charge period of eight years, with surrender charges beginning at 9% of purchase payments in the first year. Your account value in this new variable annuity is now $20,800 minus 9% of your $20,000 purchase payment, or $19,000. This is $1,000 less than you would have received if you had stayed in the original variable annuity, where you were no longer subject to surrender charges.

Ask Questions Before You Invest

Financial professionals who sell variable annuities have a duty to advise you as to whether the product they are trying to sell is suitable to your particular investment needs. Don't be afraid to ask them questions. And write down their answers, so there won't be any confusion later as to what was said.

Variable annuity contracts typically have a "free look" period of ten or more days, during which you can terminate the contract without paying any surrender charges and get back your purchase payments (which may be adjusted to reflect charges and the performance of your investment). You can continue to ask questions in this period to make sure you understand your variable annuity before the "free look" period ends.

Before you decide to buy a variable annuity, consider the following questions:

☑ Will you use the variable annuity primarily to save for retirement or a similar long-term goal?

☑ Are you investing in the variable annuity through a retirement plan or IRA (which would mean that you are not receiving any additional tax-deferral benefit from the variable annuity)?

☑ Are you willing to take the risk that your account value may decrease if the underlying mutual fund investment options perform badly?

☑ Do you understand the features of the variable annuity?

☑ Do you understand all of the fees and expenses that the variable annuity charges?

☑ Do you intend to remain in the variable annuity long enough to avoid paying any surrender charges if you have to withdraw money?

☑ If a variable annuity offers a bonus credit, will the bonus outweigh any higher fees and charges that the product may charge?

☑ Are there features of the variable annuity, such as long-term care insurance, that you could purchase more cheaply separately?

☑ Have you consulted with a tax adviser and considered all the tax consequences of purchasing an annuity, including the effect of annuity payments on your tax status in retirement?

☑ If you are exchanging one annuity for another one, do the benefits of the exchange outweigh the costs, such as any surrender charges you will have to pay if you withdraw your money before the end of the surrender charge period for the new annuity?

Remember

Before purchasing a variable annuity, you owe it to yourself to learn as much as possible about how they work, the benefits they provide, and the charges you will pay.

For More Information

You'll find on the SEC's website—www.sec.gov—a vast array of educational materials that explain how the securities industry works and provides information on avoiding costly mistakes and fraud. Some of these publications are also available in print form. To have a print brochure mailed to you, call the Federal Citizen Information Center toll-free number, (888) 878-3256. Or you can order publications online through their website, http://pueblo.gsa.gov.

☐ **Ask Questions** — Questions you should ask about all of your investments, the people who sell them to you, and what to do if you run into problems. **Available in print form**.

☐ **Saving and Investing: A Roadmap To Your Financial Security Through Saving and Investing** — Knowing how to secure your financial well-being is one of the most important things you'll ever need in life. You don't have to be a genius to do it. You just need to know a few basics, form a plan, and be ready to stick to it. No matter how much or little money you have, the important thing is to educate yourself about your opportunities. **Available in print form**.

☐ **Invest Wisely: An Introduction to Mutual Funds** — Basic information about investing in mutual funds. Much of this information applies to variable annuities, as well. **Available in print form**.

☐ **Guide for Seniors: Protect Yourself Against Investment Fraud** — Seniors are often the target of fraud. However, with some basic understanding of how scam artists work, you can avoid fraud and protect your hard-earned money. Learning how to invest safely can mean a huge difference in your retirement years. **Available in print form**.

You'll also find helpful information on these websites:

❏ **Financial Industry Regulatory Authority (FINRA)** — FINRA is an independent self-regulatory organization charged with regulating the securities industry, including sellers of variable annuities. FINRA has issued several investor alerts on the topic of variable annuities, which you can find online at www.finra.org. FINRA also periodically issues "Notices to Members," reminding them of their responsibilities to investors in selling various products, including variable annuities. If you have a complaint or problem about sales practices involving variable annuities, you should contact the District Office of FINRA nearest you. A list of FINRA District Offices is available in the "Contact Us" section of FINRA's web site at www.finra.org.

❏ **National Association of Insurance Commissioners (NAIC)** — The NAIC is the national organization of state insurance commissioners. Variable annuities are regulated by state insurance commissions, as well as by the SEC. The NAIC's web site at www.naic.org contains an interactive map of the United States with links to the home pages of each state insurance commissioner. You may contact your state insurance commissioner with questions or complaints about variable annuities.

.

Made in the USA
Columbia, SC
13 October 2021